Little Worlds

To the little worlds of Laurent, Louise, and Rachelle–GC
For my family, my friends, and their little worlds–SC

Text copyright © 2018 by Magination Press, an imprint of the American Psychological Association. Originally published in French as *Les petits mondes* by Mijade Publications (Belgium), illustrations copyright © 2017 by Sébastien Chebret, text copyright © 2017 by Géraldine Collet.

Published by
MAGINATION PRESS ® American Psychological Association
750 First Street NE, Washington, DC 20002

Magination Press is a registered trademark of the American Psychological Association.

For more information about our books, including a complete catalog, please write to us, call 1-800-374-2721, or visit our website at www.apa.org/pubs/magination.

English translation by Jenna Miley
Book design by Susan K. White
Printed by Worzalla, Stevens Point, WI

Library of Congress Cataloging-in-Publication Data
Names: Collet, Geraldine, 1975- author. | Chebret, Sebastien, 1977- illustrator.
Title: Little worlds / by Geraldine Collet ; illustrated by Sebastien Chebret.
Other titles: Petits mondes. English Description: Washington, DC : Magination Press, [2018] | «Originally published in French as Les petits mondes by Mijade Publications.»Identifiers: LCCN 2017024575| ISBN 9781433828195 (hardcover) | ISBN 1433828197 (hardcover)
Subjects: LCSH: Imagination in children—Juvenile literature.
Classification: LCC BF723.I5 C6513 2018 | DDC 153.3—dc23 LC record available at https://lccn.loc.gov/2017024575

Manufactured in the United States of America
10 9 8 7 6 5 4 3 2 1

Little Worlds

by Géraldine Collet
illustrated by Sébastien Chebret

MAGINATION PRESS • WASHINGTON, DC
American Psychological Association

HOME DÉCOR & MORE

OPEN

It's a well-known fact that everybody
has their own little world!

When Pablo wants to leave the Earth,
he climbs way up to his lair.
Perched in his treehouse,
he listens to the birds singing,
and the world below
seems even more beautiful to him.

Marion likes to build her tent
in the middle of the living room.
No one may enter without her permission…
except her cat Fifi!
Most of all, Marion loves to spend her afternoons
in her cozy palace, purring along with Fifi.

BAM!

CLANG!

Who's making all that noise?
It's Frank and Melvin!
Busy in their grandfather's workshop,
they invent machines that can do everything.
And what might this mysterious one do?

Leo loves animals so much that it's not unusual
to find him talking to them.
He is curious about everything tiny
and even the smallest ant can become his friend.

Clara escapes by watching the stars.
She travels the universe and imagines
everything she could do.
She's often told that her head is in the clouds,
and without a moment's hesitation she replies,
"Not yet, but maybe soon..."

Colors and shapes are different in Arthur's world.
He imagines the sky jumping into the sea
in a swirl of indigo and purple.
When he's asked what he sees,
he smiles because he knows
that far away, a seagull is delighted.

Watch out!
When Martin wears
his knight costume,
no dragon can escape
his cardboard sword!

A little seed here, a little seed there.
Samuel hopes that an
enormous bouquet will bloom!

As for Lili, books are what take her far away.
Every turn of the page is a new life.
So don't be surprised
if she lingers a little in the bookstore...

Marek and Simon dream of a world without war.
They hope to live in peace before they grow up.

And when they all come back from their little worlds,
they keep a wish in their hearts
to build a better one together,
here and elsewhere.

Note to Parents and Caregivers
by Julia Martin Burch, PhD

Think about when you were a child—where did you go to imagine, create, and spend time with your private hopes, dreams, and interests? What were those times like? Some of those experiences likely helped shape who you are as a person today. Whether it was spending time in the natural world, devouring books about a favorite topic, learning to work with your hands or to build things, or just using your imagination, the "little worlds" you so naturally created for yourself as a child also helped you move towards important developmental steps, such as developing imagination and creativity, learning to think flexibly and solve problems, creating a budding self-identity and sense of agency, and developing empathy for others.

As a parent, caregiver, or educator, you have a unique opportunity to nurture the development of little worlds for the children in your life. In an increasingly fast-paced and structured world, free, imaginative playtime in a special, personal space is more important than ever. By supporting your child in developing his own little world, you can help your child explore his passions, use his imagination, and contribute to his long-term development. How can you help cultivate these important skills in the children you care about? Below are some suggestions to get started.

Create time for free, imaginative play.
Unstructured playtime is an increasingly scarce commodity in our busy world. From extracurricular activities to the ubiquitous screens, children growing up today are spending less and less time engaged in free, creative play. However, unstructured play, such as the play featured in *Little Worlds*, is a critical part of a child's development. Specifically, unstructured, imaginative play helps children learn to think through and solve problems, and to develop decision-making skills. For example, as Frank and Melvin have fun building their mystery machine, they are also learning how to cooperate, as well as how to think flexibly and persevere when confronted with challenges (with no adult to swoop in and fix it for them!).

Similarly, you may have seen or heard your own child talking to themselves while in a little world of their own making. This is called "private speech" and is one of the ways in which children learn to regulate their emotions and behaviors, as well as to explore their thoughts. Private speech allows children to express their desires, emotions, and opinions out loud, as well as to guide their own behavior. For example, your child might say to herself, "stack the smaller blocks on top of the bigger blocks." Furthermore, private speech has been linked to increased motivation and focus, and more flexible and creative problem-solving skills. Time away in a little world is the ideal opportunity for children to engage in private speech, and research suggests that private speech tends to decrease rapidly once children enter elementary school.

Imaginative play also helps children develop self-regulation, or the ability to manage their emotions and behavior according to the situation. For example, when Martin pretends to be a brave knight in his little world, he is also learning to following the "rules" of his role, or how to act, talk, and think like a knight. Though it's just play now, this will be an important ability as Martin gets older and must learn to take on different roles throughout his day—such as student, sibling, and teammate—even when he might not feel like it.

So, what can you do as the adult? Create room for creativity and free play. Prioritize unstructured time for imagination among your child's other commitments and activities. You can facilitate this by making toys and activities available to your child that encourage creative play (as opposed to games with specific rules to follow). For example, finger paints, clay, building blocks, dress-up clothes, balls, and a variety of household objects offer opportunities for a child to develop her own games. Free play time outdoors is another wonderful way for children to creatively engage with their world. Encourage your child's interests and let her direct her own play. Remember how good it felt when you got to play in whatever way you wanted? Give your child the same gift. Resist the urge to step in and correct or criticize. Let Lili linger in the bookstore. Encourage Clara's imagination, rather than saying her head is in the clouds.

Foster your child's developing sense of self and identity.

Imagination and creativity open the world up to a child. Through imaginative play in her own little world, a child begins to discover her interests and passions. Over time, these interests begin to contribute to a child's overall self-identity, or understanding of herself and her role in the world. She also begins to develop a sense of agency, or the understanding that she is an independent individual with her own

hopes, feelings, thoughts, and choices.

Playtime in a safe, non-judgmental space, such as Pablo's treehouse or Marion's tent, creates an opportunity for children to try on different interests, identities, attitudes, values, and behaviors. You may recall going through various phases as an adolescent. Young children undergo a similar (though typically less dramatic!) developmental process as they begin asking "Who am I?" and move from more concrete identities, such as "I am a boy. I am four years old," to more complex identities, such as "I am a good friend and am also good at art." Whether in a tent, a hollow log, a treehouse, or some other creative place just waiting to be discovered by an inquisitive child, little worlds give children the space to explore their individuality and blossoming identity through play.

To help your child begin to build their own identity and related sense of agency, you can foster an accepting, open environment in which your child feels comfortable to try on different attitudes and interests. Be curious. Ask open-ended questions and listen more than you talk. Be respectful and supportive. If your child is like Marion and treasures her private tent space, respect her wishes and ask before you enter her little world.

Help your child build empathy.

Though the children in this story do not know each other, they offer a wonderful example of the uniqueness and the individual experiences and preferences of every person. As an adult, you likely take this fact for granted; however, a child must learn that others do not have the same thoughts, feelings, or experiences as he does. The ability to understand that the content